D1404516

America's Game

Cincinnati
Reds

CHRIS W. SEHNERT

ABDO & Daughters
PUBLISHING

Published by Abdo & Daughters, 4940 Viking Dr., Suite 622, Edina, MN 55435.

Printed in the United States.

Cover photo: Wide World Photo
Interior photos: Archive Photos, page 6
                  Wide World Photo: pages 5, 7, 11-14, 17, 20-28

Edited by Paul Joseph

Library of Congress Cataloging–in–Publication Data

Sehnert, Chris W.
    Cincinnati Reds / Chris W. Sehnert
        p. cm. — (America's game)
    Includes index.
    Summary: Focuses on some of the key players in the history of the oldest professional baseball team in America.
    ISBN 1-56239-659-5
    1. Cincinnati Reds (Baseball team)—History—Juvenile literature.
[1. Cincinnati Reds (Baseball team)—History. 2. Baseball—
History.] I. Title. II. Series.
GV875.C65S45   1996
796.357'64'0977178—dc20   95-52034
                                                      CIP
                                                      AC

Contents

The Cincinnati Reds

Cincinnati, Ohio, was the first city to have a professional baseball team. The Red Stockings' 1869 tour of American cities was the seed that grew into Major League Baseball. Today, the Cincinnati Reds play the grand old game in Riverfront Stadium, and attract thousands of cheering fans to each contest. Their history stretches from the days when a bare-handed second baseman set records for fielding, to the Gold Glove of current Reds' shortstop, Barry Larkin. In between, Cincinnati has been host to some of the greatest teams, players, and events the game has ever known. The first night game in major league history was played at Crosley Field in 1935. Three years later, Reds' pitcher Johnny Vander Meer threw not one but two no-hit games in a row!

Pete Rose, Joe Morgan, and Johnny Bench began to rewrite baseball's record book in the 1970s. During that time, the "Big Red Machine" won four National League Pennants and two World Championships. Cincinnati returned to the World Series in 1990. Led by a corps of relief pitchers nicknamed the "Nasty Boys" and starting pitcher Jose Rijo, the Reds took their fifth World Championship with a four-game sweep.

The Reds were the first champions of the new NL Central Division in 1995. Young players like Reggie Sanders and Brett Boone give Cincinnati a promising future, while the National League's 1995 Most Valuable Player, Barry Larkin, continues a tradition of greatness in professional baseball's oldest city.

Cincinnati Reds shortstop Barry Larkin leaps over a hard-sliding Pittsburgh Pirates Jay Bell.

The Cincinnati Red Stockings

Major League Baseball officially began in 1871. The Cincinnati Red Stockings started two years earlier. The game itself is older still.

Amateur baseball teams such as the Brooklyn Excelciors and Brooklyn Atlantics began to compete against one another in the 1840s. The National Association of Base Ball Players was formed in 1858 to make the rules, and set up games between its members.

After the Civil War, it was not uncommon for baseball teams to charge up to 50 cent admission for spectators to watch their games. The money earned was often split among players. Then, in 1869, the Cincinnati Red Stockings announced a tour. They would travel and play the best teams in the country.

The Cincinnati Red Stockings of 1869 were not the first team with players who were paid to play baseball. They were, however, the first team to openly admit being professional.

Presentation of a champion bat to the Cincinnati Red Stockings on their return home from a winning season.

Cincinnati businessman Aaron B. Champion provided the idea and the funds for the Red Stockings' first professional tour. The players were given uniforms which included the first use of knickers as baseball pants. This was to show off their red stockings.

The leader of the team was Harry Wright; he was both a player and manager. Wright's Red Stockings went undefeated in their first American tour, winning 60 games in a row. The next year they won their first 24 games before being knocked off by the Brooklyn Atlantics, 8-7 in 11 innings.

The Red Stockings' influence on the game continues to this day. In 1871, Harry Wright brought the team to Boston where, together with eight other clubs, they formed the first major league.

The National Association of Professional Base Ball Players lasted from 1871 to 1875. Wright's Boston Reds won the pennant four times in the league's five years of existence. His contributions to the game included equipment design, groundskeeping technique and player training. He earned the title "Father of Professional Base Ball."

The Cincinnati Red Stockings. Top row, left to right: Hurley, substitute; G. Wright, shortstop; Allison, catcher; McVey, right field; Leonard, left field. Bottom row, left to right: Sweasy, second base; Waterman, third base; Harry Wright, center field; Brainard, pitcher; Gould, first base.

The New Reds

The National League of Professional Base Ball Clubs was formed in 1876. It had eight charter organizations. The new Cincinnati Reds were one of them. Other leagues would come and go during this period, but the National League (NL) would outlast them all.

The new Reds finished dead last in their first two seasons. In 1878, they went 37-28 to finish in second place, four games behind Harry Wright's Boston Red Stockings. They were led by the hitting of Charley "Baby" Jones, and the pitching of Will "Whoop-la" White.

The Reds fell back to last place in 1880. After the season, they dropped out of the league. In 1881, there was no professional baseball in Cincinnati.

The NL began getting competition in 1882. The American Association (AA) was formed, and proved to be a considerable rival. Having sat out for a season, the Cincinnati Reds organization became one of six teams to join the new league. Will White returned, and carried the Reds to a pennant-winning 55-25 season. White led the AA in several pitching categories including wins (40), complete games (52), and shutouts (8).

After the season, the Reds played two exhibition games with the NL champion Chicago White Stockings. The two-game series was a split. It was a prelude to the first World Series.

King Bid

The pennant-winning Reds of 1882 featured rookie second baseman John "Bid" McPhee. "King Bid," as he was known, was a small man. He stood 5 feet, 8 inches tall and weighed 152 pounds.

McPhee led the American Association in fielding his rookie season with a .920 fielding percentage. He went on to play 18 seasons with the Reds, and led the league in fielding 7 more times.

Amazingly, seven of his eight fielding titles were won with his bare hands! In the 1880s, players began wearing gloves as standard equipment. "Bid" refused to comply. When he started the 1896 season with a sore finger, he finally gave in. The result was a .978 fielding percentage that not only led the league, but remains among the highest of all-time.

McPhee retired after the 1899 season, and became the Reds' manager. His 6,545 putouts are a major league record to this day. He was the greatest second baseman of the 19th century.

The Reds continued to field winning teams, but would not win another pennant for several years. Meanwhile, the influx of rival professional baseball leagues was weakening the American Association. In 1890, the Cincinnati Reds jumped back to the NL where they continue to reside today.

The Modern Era Begins

The American League (AL) began play in 1900, and signaled the arrival of baseball's modern era. The NL did not immediately recognize the new league as its equal.

The Cincinnati Reds finished last in the 1901 NL race. Owner John T. Brush responded by selling the team. The new ownership was headed by August "Garry" Herrmann.

Herrmann was instrumental in developing a truce between the rival leagues. He became the chairperson for the newly formed National Commission. The first modern-day World Series would be played in 1903.

Player-manager Joe Kelley and outfielder Cy Seymour starred for the Reds in the early part of the century. In 1905, Seymour took the NL's batting crown (.377), and the runs batted in (RBI) crown (121). His eight home runs (HRs) left him one short of becoming the NL's first modern-day Triple Crown winner. Despite his efforts, the Reds finished 26 games out of first.

The Reds traded for two future Hall of Famers in 1916. The New York Giants sent them Christy Mathewson and Edd Roush. Mathewson pitched just one game for the Reds. It was the last of the 373 wins in his spectacular career. Roush's outstanding career was just getting started.

Reds See Black

The Reds added pitchers Slim Sallee and Ray Fisher in 1919, and brought Cincinnati its first pennant in 37 years. Roush won his second batting title in three years, and finished second in RBIs with 71. Sallee finished the season with 21 wins. The Reds went 96-44, and finished 9 games ahead of the Giants.

Cincinnati defeated the Chicago White Sox in the 1919 World Series. Their victory was tainted by the darkest scandal in the history of Major League Baseball. Eight White Sox players had conspired with gamblers to purposely lose baseball's World Series.

Judge Kenesaw Mountain Landis was appointed as the first Commissioner of Baseball. His job was to restore the public's faith in the game. The eight players involved in the scandal were given lifetime banishment from professional baseball. Among them was

the great "Shoeless" Joe Jackson. He and his seven teammates would forever be referred to as the "Black Sox."

Chicago White Sox player "Shoeless" Joe Jackson, considered by many to be one of the greatest natural hitters of all time.

The first major league night game, played in 1935 between the Reds and Philadelphia Phillies. The Reds won 2-1.

Reds Light Up The Night

The Reds hired Leland "Larry" MacPhail to run the organization in 1933. MacPhail had experience working for a minor league baseball organization in Columbus, Ohio. He drew on the experience to bring night baseball to the major league level.

MacPhail's first move was to convince Cincinnati industrialist Powell Crosley, Jr., to invest in the club. Crosley and MacPhail persuaded the other NL owners to allow Cincinnati to play seven night games in 1935.

On May 24, 1935, the lights came on at Crosley Field. The switch was thrown from the White House by United States President Franklin Delano Roosevelt. The Reds defeated the Philadelphia Phillies, 2-1, in front of 20,000 fans.

Overall, the Reds attendance in 1935 was twice that of the previous season. In a few short years, profits at the box office would translate into a winning team.

Once In A Lifetime

Bill McKechnie was hired to manage the Reds in 1938. Catcher Ernie "The Schnozz" Lombardi won the 1938 batting title (.342), and was elected the NL's Most Valuable Player (MVP). Frank McCormick led the league in hits (209), and finished fourth in RBIs (106).

Paul Derringer, Bucky Walters, and Johnny Vander Meer anchored the Reds' pitching staff. Derringer and Walters were right-handers. Vander Meer was left-handed. His historic accomplishment in June 1938 is unlikely to ever be duplicated.

Vander Meer pitched a no-hit shutout over the Boston Braves on June 11, 1938. This rare achievement of total domination is, normally, a once-in-a-lifetime experience for a pitcher. But not for this pitcher.

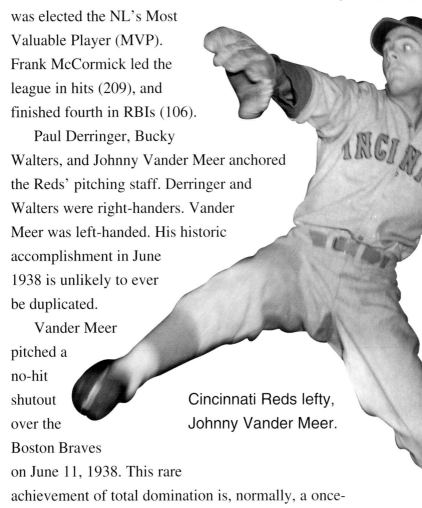

Cincinnati Reds lefty, Johnny Vander Meer.

Vander Meer's next start was in Brooklyn four days later. June 15, 1938 was to be a historic night for Dodger baseball. Larry MacPhail had brought lights to Ebbets Field, just as he had done in Cincinnati three years earlier. The stadium was jammed with 40,000 fans who witnessed the debut of night baseball in New York. What they saw was the rarest of all baseball feats.

Johnny Vander Meer kept the Dodgers loose with his characteristic wildness and a sizzling fastball. He was unhittable through seven innings when he began to tire. Realizing his pitcher was wearing thin, Lombardi began calling for the curve, and Vandy delivered with strikes.

In the ninth inning, with a 6-0 lead and his no-hitter intact, Vander Meer began to lose control. He walked the bases loaded before a force out at the plate brought him one out away. Brooklyn's Leo Durocher pinch-hit, and slammed a pitch into the upper deck— just foul! His line-out to center completed Vander Meer's incredible back-to-back no-hit wonder.

In New York's first night game, Johnny Vander Meer fires a pitch during his 6-0 no-hit win against Brooklyn.

Return To Glory

Despite the heroics of the 1938 season, the Reds finished six games behind the Chicago Cubs in the NL pennant race. They returned in 1939 to bring Cincinnati the first of two-straight NL titles.

The 1939 Reds were again powered by a dominant pitching staff. Vander Meer was lost to a shoulder injury early in the season. Derringer and Walters picked up the slack. Walters turned in a rare Triple Crown performance, leading the NL in wins (27), ERA (2.29), and strikeouts (137). Paul Derringer was Walters' closest competitor in wins (25), and led the league in winning percentage (.711).

The Reds took hold of first place in May, and carried it all the way to their first pennant in 20 years. They finished four-and-a-half games ahead of the St. Louis Cardinals, and met the New York Yankees in the World Series.

The Yankees were led by Joe DiMaggio. The "Yankee Clipper" along with rookie Charlie Keller blasted the Reds in a four-game sweep of the World Series. It was the Yankees second-straight Series sweep, and fourth-consecutive World Championship.

The 1940 season had a happier ending for the Reds. They breezed through the NL schedule winning 100 games, and a second-straight pennant. This time they defeated the Detroit Tigers in a "seesaw" World Series that went seven games.

Cincinnati fans would have to wait another 21 years before a return to the "Fall Classic." Ernie Lombardi retired with a career .306 batting average and 990 RBIs. He and Reds' manager Bill McKechnie were both inducted into the Baseball Hall of Fame.

Mr. Robinson

Frank Robinson joined the Reds in 1956. He hit 38 homers that year to tie a major league record for rookies. He was named the NL Rookie of the Year, and the Reds enjoyed their first winning season in 12 years.

The 1961 Reds were paced by Frank Robinson's MVP season, in which he batted .323, had 37 HRs, and 124 RBIs. He was joined in the outfield by Vada Pinson, who led the league in hits (208), and finished second in the batting race (.343) behind Pittsburgh's Roberto Clemente (.351). The pitching staff included Joey Jay, who was traded to the Reds by the Milwaukee Braves. Jay proved to be a vital acquisition, as he led the NL in wins (21) and shutouts (4) in his first season with Cincinnati.

The Reds won the 1961 NL Pennant by four games over the Dodgers, who had moved to Los Angeles in 1958. They faced a familiar World Series opponent in the New York Yankees.

The powerful Yankees dispatched the Reds in five games. Whitey Ford claimed two victories for the New Yorkers with 14 innings of shutout pitching. The Reds' only victory came in Game 2, as Jay limited the Yankees to four hits.

Frank Robinson's career in Cincinnati ended with an all-star season in 1965. He was traded to the Baltimore Orioles where he won the AL's MVP with a Triple Crown season in 1966.

Robinson hit 586 career home runs, placing him fourth on the all-time list. In 1975, he became the first black manager in the major leagues. He was elected to the Hall of Fame in 1982.

Facing page: Frank Robinson gets a handshake from teammate Ted Kluszewski after crossing home plate.

Cincinnati

Johny Vander Meer pitched back-to-back no hitters in 1938.

Catcher Johnny Bench, 1968 Rookie of the Year.

Frank Robinson hit 38 homers in 1956, his first year with the Reds, tying a major league record for rookies.

Reds

In 1972 second baseman Joe Morgan led the NL with 122 runs.

In his first 10 years in the major leagues, Barry Larkin has been an All-Star 7 times.

Pete Rose slapped his 4,190th base hit in 1984, breaking Ty Cobb's record.

Brett Boone finished the 1995 season with 28 home runs, 99 RBIs, and 36 stolen bases.

Piece By Piece

While Robinson was bringing World Championships to Baltimore, the Reds were building a dynasty.

Pete Rose, a Cincinnati native nicknamed "Charlie Hustle," was Rookie of the Year in 1963. Tony Perez arrived from Cuba in 1964, and Johnny Bench was named Rookie of the Year in 1968.

In 1969 (the first year of divisional play), the Reds finished four games out of first in the NL Western division. The next season they moved into Riverfront Stadium, and began a decade of dominance.

Reds' catcher Johnny Bench, 1968 Rookie of the Year.

The Big Red Machine

The 1970 Reds won 102 games under their new manager, George "Sparky" Anderson. Cincinnati took the Western Division by 14.5 games, and were dubbed the "Big Red Machine." They won three-straight games over the Pittsburgh Pirates in the NL Championship Series to win the pennant.

The 1970 World Series matched the young Reds against the veteran Baltimore Orioles. Frank Robinson hit two home runs in the Series, but it was another Robinson that did in the Reds.

Brooks Robinson's outstanding defensive play at third base continually squelched the Reds' attempted rallies. At the plate, he was equally devastating. He was named the World Series MVP as Baltimore beat Cincinnati in five games.

The Phillies' Mike Schmidt slides into second base in a cloud of dust but is tagged out by the Reds' Joe Morgan.

The Reds were NL Champions again in 1972. They were strengthened by the addition of Joe Morgan at second base. Morgan had come from the Houston Astros in an off-season trade.

The 1972 NL offensive leader board was very Red. Rose led the league in hits (198), Morgan led the league in runs (122), and Bench topped the charts in HRs (40) and RBIs (125). They won the Western Division by 10.5 games over Houston, and beat the Pirates in the playoffs.

The Reds ran into the AL's new dynasty in the World Series. The Oakland Athletics, with pitchers Jim "Catfish" Hunter, Vida Blue, and Rollie Fingers, took their first of three-straight World Championships. It was a tightly contested seven-game Series. Six of the games were decided by one run.

Reds' second baseman Joe Morgan goes up on his toes to avoid a slide by Los Angeles Dodgers' Dave Lopes. Morgan's throw to first caught Dodgers' batter Bill Russell to complete a double play.

On To Victory

The Big Red Machine cruised to their third pennant of the decade in 1975. Their 108 victories was a franchise record that still stands. The entire Reds infield was made up of all-stars!

The awesome lineup included Tony Perez at first, Joe Morgan at second, Dave Concepcion at shortstop, Pete Rose at third, and Johnny Bench behind the plate. Two of the outfielders, Ken Griffey and George Foster, would make the All-Star Team the following year.

The 1975 World Series was a classic. The Reds met the Boston Red Sox for a seven-game struggle that featured 13 home runs and several defensive gems. Boston's Carlton Fisk hit a foul-pole shot at Fenway Park which ended Game 6 in the bottom of the 12th inning. The Reds recovered to take Game 7 and their first World Championship in 35 years.

Pete Rose dives into third in the ninth inning of Game 7 of the 1975 World Series.

The Reds finished the 1976 season with 102 victories. Rose led the NL in hits (215), doubles (42) and runs (130). George Foster led the league in RBIs (121), and Joe Morgan was named the NL's MVP for the second year in a row.

In the post-season, the Big Red Machine was unbeatable. They swept the Philadelphia Phillies (3-0) in the NL Championship Series. It was their fourth pennant in seven years.

The Reds followed their playoff sweep by destroying the New York Yankees in the 1976 World Series. The Reds became the first NL team in 54 years to repeat as World Champions.

Above: Pitcher Will McEnaney is carried by catcher Johnny Bench as Pete Rose joins the fun after winning Game 7 of the 1975 World Series.

Right: Fans run onto the field to help the Reds celebrate their World Series victory.

All Things Must Pass

The Reds won the NL's Western Division again in 1979. They were defeated in the playoffs by the Pittsburgh Pirates. The conclusion of the 1970s brought an end to the Reds' dynasty.

The age of free-agency had begun. Pete Rose, Joe Morgan and Sparky Anderson all left Cincinnati. The Big Red Machine was a memory as Cincinnati did not win a pennant in the 1980s.

Johnny Bench played his entire career with the Reds. He retired after the 1983 season as the all-time home run leader among catchers. His career included two NL MVP Awards (1970, 1972), and 14 All-Star selections. He was inducted into the Hall of Fame in 1989.

Joe Morgan retired after the 1984 season. His 22-year career was the longest of any major league second baseman. He was inducted into the Baseball Hall of Fame in 1990.

Pete Rose returned to the Reds as a player-manager in 1984. The next year he slapped his 4,190th base hit. This career highlight moved him in front of Ty Cobb as Major League Baseball's "Hit King."

Rose's reign came to an unfortunate conclusion. In 1989, Commissioner A. Bartlett Giamatti banished him from the major leagues. It was discovered Rose had placed bets on baseball games. The man who has played in more major league games, and collected more hits than any other person, is currently ineligible for the Hall of Fame.

Back On Top

The banishment of Pete Rose left the Reds in need of new leadership. Owner Marge Schott hired Lou Piniella to manage the team in 1990. Piniella brought welcomed results after the disasters of 1989.

The Reds started the season with nine-straight victories. They held onto their lead throughout the season, and won the Western division by five games over the Los Angeles Dodgers.

Outstanding relief pitching from Randy Myers, Norm Charlton, and Rob Dibble paved the way for Cincinnati's success. The three bullpen mates were nicknamed "The Nasty Boys" for their aggressive pitching style.

The Reds knocked off the powerful Pittsburgh Pirates in the 1990 NL Championship to win the Pennant. The Oakland Athletics swept the Boston Red Sox in the AL Championship to win their third Pennant in a row. The Athletics won 103 games in 1990, and were heavily favored to repeat as World Champions.

The Reds were sparked by outfielder Billy Hatcher's record-setting seven-consecutive hits in the first two games of the World Series. Chris Sabo launched two homers in Game 3, and Jose Rijo pitched a gem in Game 4 to complete the sweep for Cincinnati.

The Reds' fifth World Championship had arrived unexpectedly. It completed a season of relief for fans of the Cincinnati ball club.

Up To Date

Today the Reds remain one of the NL's premier teams. They became the first team to win the NL's new Central Division in 1995. They were defeated in the playoffs by the World Champion Atlanta Braves.

Cincinnati's Barry Larkin is the league's top shortstop. He leads the Reds with a combination of stellar defense, solid hitting, and lightning speed. In his first 10 years in the major leagues, he has been an All-Star 7 times. He was named the NL's MVP in 1995.

Reggie Sanders and Brett Boone are two of the Reds' most consistent young players. Boone's father, Bob, and grandfather, Ray, both played Major League Baseball. Sanders completed the 1995 season among the NL leaders in HRs (28), RBIs (99), and stolen bases (36).

Cincinnati, Ohio, is a city that has witnessed baseball's growth from the time players were first paid to play. It has been host to some of baseball's greatest players and teams. World Champions, Hall of Famers, and all-time leaders; Cincinnati has been home to them all. The Cincinnati Reds and Major League Baseball have grown up together, and the relationship continues to this day.

Reds' second baseman Brett Boone shows off the ball after tagging Chicago Cubs' Sammy Sosa on an attempt to steal second.

Glossary

All-Star: A player who is voted by fans as the best player at one position in a given year.

American League (AL): An association of baseball teams formed in 1900 which make up one-half of the major leagues.

American League Championship Series (ALCS): A best-of-seven-game playoff with the winner going to the World Series to face the National League Champions.

Batting Average: A baseball statistic calculated by dividing a batter's hits by the number of times at bat.

Earned Run Average (ERA): A baseball statistic which calculates the average number of runs a pitcher gives up per nine innings of work.

Fielding Average: A baseball statistic which calculates a fielder's success rate based on the number of chances the player has to record an out.

Hall of Fame: A memorial for the greatest baseball players of all time located in Cooperstown, New York.

Home Run (HR): A play in baseball where a batter hits the ball over the outfield fence scoring everyone on base as well as the batter.

Major Leagues: The highest ranking associations of professional baseball teams in the world, currently consisting of the American and National Baseball Leagues.

Minor Leagues: A system of professional baseball leagues at levels below Major League Baseball.

National League (NL): An association of baseball teams formed in 1876 which make up one-half of the major leagues.

National League Championship Series (NLCS): A best-of-seven-game playoff with the winner going to the World Series to face the American League Champions.

Pennant: A flag which symbolizes the championship of a professional baseball league.

Pitcher: The player on a baseball team who throws the ball for the batter to hit. The pitcher stands on a mound and pitches the ball toward the strike zone area above the plate.

Plate: The place on a baseball field where a player stands to bat. It is used to determine the width of the strike zone. Forming the point of the diamond-shaped field, it is the final goal a base runner must reach to score a run.

RBI: A baseball statistic standing for *runs batted in.* Players receive an RBI for each run that scores on their hits.

Rookie: A first-year player, especially in a professional sport.

Slugging Percentage: A statistic which points out a player's ability to hit for extra bases by taking the number of total bases hit and dividing it by the number of at bats.

Stolen Base: A play in baseball when a base runner advances to the next base while the pitcher is delivering his pitch.

Strikeout: A play in baseball when a batter is called out for failing to put the ball in play after the pitcher has delivered three strikes.

Triple Crown: A rare accomplishment when a single player finishes a season leading their league in batting average, home runs, and RBIs. A pitcher can win a Triple Crown by leading the league in wins, ERA, and strikeouts.

Walk: A play in baseball when a batter receives four pitches out of the strike zone and is allowed to go to first base.

World Series: The championship of Major League Baseball played since 1903 between the pennant winners from the American and National Leagues.

Index